Prose on the Path

A Journey of Self Discovery

Carrie Coppola

To Tony who continually encourages, endlessly inspires,
is forever my ally!

The path . . .

A deep longing lives in each of us to know who we truly are. Once we acknowledge and accept that desire, we put ourselves on the path. Accepting the longing, the path opens to us, we are welcomed there. As we seek understanding of Self, we are given guidance and direction, we learn to live in alignment with our truth, know what we value, discover our purpose.

Being on the path takes courage and deep willingness. We will inevitably be led through twists and turns, guided into uncharted territory, over treacherous terrain, across the most spectacular valleys. No matter what we encounter, the signposts are there, continually directing us home, toward our true north.

The path leads us to develop a deep sense of trust in our journey. A sense that no matter what we uncover, no matter what is revealed, it is there for our highest good. Yes, we will encounter things we have tried to avoid or deny, yet when we stay, go where the path leads us, we discover qualities that support our journey, qualities that have been covered, have been forgotten, have not been realized. Qualities such presence, patience, wisdom, trust, surrender.

Continuing to trust our path, more and more will be revealed. Our task is to persist!

My path . . .

A renewed commitment to continue on my path opened for me at a profound moment in my life. I found myself on precarious terrain. I felt unprepared for the sudden turns my life had taken – divorce, my son struggling, physical constraints. I was depressed, anxious, my world felt shattered. Feeling all the emotions of being disconnected from self – fear, loneliness, sadness, insecurity - I was seeking direction, seeking guidance home. Rather than listening to the voice that said stop, turn and run (a pattern of fear), I remained on my path. Having no idea how to navigate this new terrain, I could feel the yearning inside. I listened to my heart, knew I was ready for deeper healing, ready to be found. Grace moved me forward.

My path was already filled with many practices supporting my journey – recovery, meditation, journaling, prayer, therapy. Though the path felt wide and expansive, something was missing. I trusted that feeling. I allowed the surety of my readiness to lead me forward. I allowed myself to see the signs. The path opened for me. Yoga found me there.

Yoga held me in a time of some of my deepest healing, led me to the depths of my woundedness. What yoga added to my path was a deep connection to my body. After years of dissociating any time a challenge arose, any time my trauma was triggered, it felt profound to remain in the moment, to embody the present. To learn how to feel, truly feel what the moment was offering was miraculous. Yoga gave me room to stay with me and my experience. To stay long enough to find me! To discover a bravery to heal my trauma. Layer by layer, long hidden secrets were revealed, long held pain was exposed. Yoga gave me room to be in my wholeness, to accept all of me, fully embrace my shadow, and just as importantly my radiance.

Over time, my path opened wider. After going to school and working my dream job, I was guided to change careers. My path led me to become a yoga teacher, to open a yoga studio, and to eventually close that studio. All these possibilities were offered to me by staying on my path, by allowing the qualities I possess to rise in the moment, by trusting the process!

The gifts I have received are plentiful, abundant. A few are my ability to be present, to feel a sense of true belonging, to have a renewed relationship with myself filled with compassion, trust, and fierce, powerful love. That is the beauty the path gives to me. To stand in my truth, in my body, to receive clarity, is nothing less than amazing. To listen to my soul's longings, to hear from my heart, and take action toward it is profound. My path is continually giving me those extraordinary moments in the midst of my ordinary life.

Our path . . .

This book is a compilation of writings that have arisen from being on my path. Allowing myself to be found, my writing was birthed. I allowed my experiences to pour through my heart onto the page. Each prose gives you a window into my experience of learning how to live in alignment with my true self, and the many ways I forget that! A window into how the path gives me room to understand me, to know what I value, what I believe and how to stand more fully in my belonging. To know I am enough and in the same moment, a work in progress!

This book contains yoga and its teachings, yet it is not a book about yoga. Rather, it is a book about what happens when you create room for your practices, when you commit yourself to your path. It is a book about how your life may open when you make room to know you. It is a book, an offering, for us all to expand and evolve in the most magical ways.

I share my experiences with you to connect to your path, to your truest self. To find room for yourself to take the brave risk of being you. Wholly and fully you in the world! To know what is at your core, to listen to your soul and ignite the passions that want to come alive within you. To embrace the full spectrum of you being human.

Prose on the Path

These prose are personal experiences, a sharing of my heart, that emerged through me over many years.

My hope is that the timeless nature of my musings reminds you that you're never truly alone. That as you read them, the invitation to connect to that deep part of you, your soul longing to be heard, listened to, understood, is accepted. That the connection to your soul awakens the brave, courageous you, the you ready to heal, the you ready to discover who you truly are. That you may recognize your essence and rise to your most emPowered, authentic self.

With each writing, I offer simple ways to connect with them more deeply: through contemplation, breath, actions. It's the ABCs, turned upside down — a set of practices to keep the writing alive and to help you create an ongoing narrative to live by . . .

C: *Contemplation* to delve deeper in your process. To allow spaces to open, to look beyond the barriers erected out of protection, to create room for inspiration, direct experiences of you and your truth. To witness your fears, your doubts, your worries and see beyond the façade that tells you these limitations are not in the way. To allow you to be a seeker, guided by that inherent need to know Self. To let contemplation be an everyday experience.

B: *Breath* practices to center, ground, align you in the moment.

Breath to empower you to soften your heart, find your voice, to be whole. Breath to realize this potent super power is at your fingertips in every given day, in every given moment. Breath to make your life deeper, richer, more exquisite than you can imagine. Breath to receive your life force coursing, connecting, conveying the truth that you are made of star stuff, moon beams, beautiful trajectories of light.

A: *Actions* to guide you to experience yourself as emPowered!

To bring to life all of your experiences. Actions to let your life be a fully lived experience. Actions to walk the walk!! To demonstrate your bravery, your willingness to live out loud. Actions to lead you to embody the truth that you belong, that you are enough, powerful beyond measure. Actions to know that you have a place here.

I hope to reciprocate the generosity of the gifts my path has given me -in my living, in my teachings, in my interactions, and here, in my words.

May they show you how you are ready!
May they expand your path in ways that surprise and delight.
May we know we are all on the collective path to joy.

Beginnings often frighten us because they seem like lonely voyages into the unknown. Yet, in truth, no beginning is empty or isolated. We seem to think that beginning is setting out from a lonely point along some line of direction into the unknown. This is not the case. Shelter and energy come alive when a beginning is embraced... We are never as alone in our beginnings as it might seem at the time.
- John O'Donohue

I wrote this first prose as a new year was upon us. The new year is the beginning we all know, even get excited about. My experience has shown the glamour of that wears off fast! This writing is an invitation to see beginnings as an everyday experience, one that we are 'sheltered' in, held in, supported in. One that is guiding us toward possibilities beyond our imagination, if we will just begin.

BEGINNING

There is much anticipation in a beginning. All the old ways of being behind us, the things that did not quite turn out the way we wanted, all the 'should have' moments and the 'could have' times released. We step into any new beginning with great eagerness and excitement, an open path before us. Our body tingles with the joy of hope; we feel giddy with the new. Then another sensation arises – that old familiar ting, the tension and stress holding our fear of opening, our fear of beginning. Often that dread wins out over the enthusiasm, and we find ourselves never finishing what we began, not even ever really beginning. We let go before our process starts.

My experience is that many of us hold a negative connotation of a being a beginner. We think we are supposed to already know how to do what we are beginning. We desire to bypass that frightening, vulnerable place of being at the start of something. We want to skip the part where we are wobbly or bumbling in front of the world. We desire to come out of the shoot cooked, done, already at the place we have envisioned at the onset. We fear this place of in-between so much that we are even willing to pick up those old ways of being that we were so ready to let go of and convince ourself it was not really so bad after all. We allow the old beliefs to shroud our fear and hold ourselves back from the beautiful place of possibility, the exquisite process a beginning offers us.

As much, and as hard as we try to resist beginnings, they are happening all the time. Some we choose; others are chosen for us. Each beginning is a new opportunity for us to be here, fully present, a place of arising. In the Zen Buddhist tradition, there is a concept called Beginners Mind – a state where we stand on the edge our experience, released of expectations, free of how it should be, detached from any intended outcome. That place holds a freshness, a brand-newness, moments waiting to happen, waiting to be. In the same instance, it holds for us incredible vulnerability as it encompasses the unknown. The practice of yoga is the perfect laboratory to examine our relationship with this vulnerability, to expand our practice and connect to how we hold ourselves back from beginning, from being a beginner.

Our mat offers us beginnings, possibility, places of initiation. A place to let the pose be brand new, the moment be fresh so that we can experience it exactly as it is and receive the benefits that the present is offering us. Each time we return to mountain pose, each time we bow in child's pose, we are asked to let go of what just occurred and extend ourselves fresh, renewed, as we begin again. We are also given an opportunity to acknowledge our direct experience and the messiness, awkwardness we may have experienced as we try a new pose, a subtle adjustment, or even what our old familiar poses offer us in that moment. It gives room for us to step into that vulnerable place of the unknown and feel the ground will be there for us. There we find the power to transform. Power to become more courageous. To become more fully who we are. A place that contains the potential to embrace vulnerability.

Embracing vulnerability deepens in the opportunity to share our whole experience. Often our process is skipped over. We talk only of 'this happened and now I am here.' We leave out the middle – the moment when we begin, the moment when we must step, and our fear arises. The moments where we show ourselves fully as we learn, when the right word is not spoken, when we make a mistake in front of everyone, when we are clumsy, inexperienced, gawky. The moment we stand in the world in our less than perfect form, revealing our most real, true self. We have an opportunity on our yoga mat to be in that process – the start, the vulnerable middle, the messiness, the completion, the other side. Our practice can help us come into acceptance of the process of our growth. To be the brave, authentic being, willing to share the whole story, not just the parts we think will be acceptable in the world – all in an effort to support each other toward the beginnings, toward the invitations waiting. All in an effort to be in our wholeness.

In many stores or places of business, a new clerk will wear an 'in training' tag. Wearing the tag, they are treated with compassion, understanding, and forgiveness in a way that we do not normally express to each other. They are forgiven when they do not do things correctly, are seen with compassion for their laborious learning, and are held in understanding as they begin. As soon as that badge is removed, our expectations go up, and they must operate according to our standards.

The truth is that we are all 'in training,' beginning our next new thing, new adventure, new relationship, new grief, new joy. 'In training' when we take a risk and follow our heart's calling, to begin despite our fears. 'In training' when our world as we know it falls apart. 'In training' when we show up in the world exactly as we are, released from having the perfect words to say, from our desire to prove ourself, from our need to be accepted. 'In training' for this next new moment that is right before us.

The teachings of yoga offer us this place; it is what the practice gives us again and again – a condition of beginning, a freshness, unencumbered by the myriad of ways we protect ourself from the unknown. It offers us a place to stay in the tingly, giddiness, unafraid to show our excitement, brave to be revealed in our unknowing, bold to be a beginner in front of all. It gives us all a place to wear our 'in training' badge with honor, starting from a place where we are already enough, already belong, are loved beyond belief.

May we all feel the possibility of being 'in training.' Not the perfected, put-together, has all the answers, us. Rather the real, messy, unkept, raw, true beginners. From that place, may we expand in to this new place, with exuberance to be revealed in who we are, see the beginning as an opportunity, of fertile ground to stand in our truth. There, I invite you to stand with me, heart open, held in compassion, love, and understanding, ready for your beginning, knowing that we are all on this journey, 'in training' to be JOY! And there to begin again, and again, and again.

The last year or so has been one of beginnings for me. Interestingly, I believe I have been more focused on the ending rather than any beginning. That may arise from being unclear on what is before me. All I do know is that there is a beginning before me. That makes it feel even more vulnerable, more precarious. Yet, what a beautiful opportunity to step even more bravely toward it. To not have to know, not have to figure it out. To be in this present moment, allowing myself to begin here without knowing what I am beginning! I believe that is called surrender!

Contemplation to delve deeper in your process:

Write about an experience of beginning. Make much room for the middle! Give it description, honor this essential part of your process, embrace your vulnerability. Tell the story of the unspoken.

Then, write about what you are ready to begin. Affirm this to yourself: I will allow the whole process of this beginning to be embraced, knowing it is a vital part of the story!

Breath practices to center, ground, align you in the moment:

Simple counted breath, a beautiful place to begin. Start from a place of compassion, letting go of expectations. Find a comfortable seat. Begin to find your breath, breath in through the nose, out through the nose. Breathe in 1 2 3; breathe out 1 2 3. Continue inhaling, exhaling, counting. Complete 6 rounds, working up to one minute. Notice what you are ready to begin.

Actions to guide you to experience yourself as emPowered!

With your contemplation on your experience of beginning complete, share it with your most trusted soul person, one who is deserving of hearing your story.

Stand in Mountain Pose, bow in child's pose – affirm:

I am beginning, I open to all that beginning offers me.
I release my expectations, my perfectionism.
I know I am enough.

Make an 'in training' badge! Decorate it. Make it yours. Place it on your altar, hang it on your wall, post it on your computer, tape it to your mirror. Let it be a beautiful reminder that you are deserving of compassion, understanding, and forgiveness.

II

We shall not cease from exploration
And the end of all our exploring
Will be to arrive where we started
And know the place for the first time.
- T.S. Eliot

Many years have passed since I put pen to paper about these experiences. Two prose that were each turning points for me. They exposed my defenses, which then became less obtrusive. I began to feel safe enough to go deeper into the experiences of my life. An expedition I had not planned for, yet had been packing for my whole life. An expedition that took an unpacking to be explored. I am grateful for these explorations – for all they have brought, and all they have yet to reveal. Arriving at the moment. All of us.

MY JOURNEY

My journey begins with a poem - The Journey by David Whyte:

Above the mountains
the geese turn into
the light again

Painting their
black silhouettes
on an open sky.

Sometimes everything
has to be
inscribed across
the heavens

so you can find
the one line
already written
inside you.

Sometimes it takes
a great sky
to find that

first, bright
and indescribable
wedge of freedom
in your own heart.

Sometimes with
the bones of the black
sticks left when the fire

has gone out

someone has written
something new
in the ashes of your life.

You are not leaving.
Even as the light fades quickly now,
you are arriving.

    I was inspired to write the words of this poem on a blank piece of white paper. I folded the paper neatly into a card and placed it inconspicuously in my son Tony's backpack as he ventured off on his journey to the other side of the world. His destinations were uncertain, his walking forward inevitable, his peace with the journey certain.

    The poem was an invitation for him to greet every day as it arrived. I wanted myself to do the same, and I believed that in that space, my peace was certain. However, as the first day turned into the first week, I began to realize the extent that I was not at peace. His own 'arriving' quickly changed to his 'leaving.' I found myself in a place longing for what had been. My grasp so tight, my suffering inevitable, my peace so distant.

    With my peace so distant, so uncertain, David Whyte's profound words began to come alive for me – this was my arriving, my journey. Gratefully, my mat called to me, and I began to deepen my yoga practice. I came to my mat and observed the way that yoga was expanding in my life by allowing me this opportunity to re-discover my true nature, to be at peace with me, to be at peace with the world, to be at peace with Tony's journey.

    Day after day the practices began to crack me open. My journey, focusing inward, revealed the place my discomfort stemmed, what I was grasping, where I was in denial and disconnected from Source. The more time on my mat, the quieter I became. The quieter I became, the more inward focused I was. I moved toward silence and listened. My deepened introspection allowed my vision to clear.

New awareness and deep shifts began to take place. Shifts where I could begin to recognize my fears, my misperceptions, my limited beliefs. Those ranged from wanting our relationship to remain the same, to a space of waiting, being on hold until he returned. The next layer held even deeper fears – fears of losing him, losing our relationship, losing my identity.

As uncomfortable as all of this was to face, my practice brought me to a space where I could be content with feeling and experiencing this darkness, my shadow. An even deeper contentment arose as I took that experience off the mat and began writing about it, talking about it. Little by slowly, my view of this experience transformed, no longer bound by the constant pull of my expectations and fears. In that space, I experienced a release as I allowed myself to feel what was beyond the fear – sadness, anger, longing, loneliness. I was then free to experience how much I missed our daily contact. This softening opened my heart to experience the deep, amazing love that I feel for him, the pride I felt for his adventurous spirit, the profound connection our hearts hold – a connection beyond miles and oceans.

I would love to say that peace was certain at each stage, but that would not be true. What I can say is that I discovered through my journey into the dark, into the ashes, that beautiful wedge of freedom in my own heart. I re-discovered the line already written inside me – in the journey of arriving peace is certain.

I am very grateful for Tony, whose courage and strength to begin his journey allowed me to begin this new phase of my journey, my arriving – every day arriving.

There will be so many moments after this that I help my son pack his bags for his next adventure. His latest adventure: a move to a new city to start a new life. A bit more permanent this time. As I look back at the time of this writing, I realize this was simply a preparation for me. A planting of a seed, an opening of a journey that would bring me so many more opportunities to be in a space of arrival. So many more opportunities to grow peace. The layers are still there for me to discover; the attachments still linger. Yet, I know this is a beautiful opportunity to discover me, to arrive at my own heart, in my own new way to be in the world. The hole left from this last year of letting go of that which is very close to my heart is being filled with new connections, dreams, opportunities, spirit – in other words, all forms of love! I am arriving, right here, right now, trusting the journey, rediscovering the certainty of peace.

Contemplation to delve deeper in your process:

What is arriving at the door of your heart? What are the layers waiting for you to discover? Where are you grasping, clinging, attached? What does peace feel like in your body? What does it look like in your life?

Breath practices to center, ground, align you in the moment:

emPowered breath. Find a comfortable seat. Begin to find your breath, breath in through the nose, out through the nose. Next inhale, draw your breath into the belly. At the completion of your inhale, retain your breath – visualize a beautiful yellow stream spiraling inward. Receive stability, balance. Exhale slowly, allowing the energy to flow through all parts of you – visualize an infinite well of vitality in your belly. A place you can draw nourishment whenever you need. Repeat twice (working up to six rounds).

Actions to guide you to experience yourself as emPowered!

After the reflections in Contemplation, move your experience through your body (cat/cow, hip circles, cobra flow, arm circles). As you embrace the sensations, begin to notice any emotions arising. Give yourself time to sit with each of them. Now talk about it. Let this process be a part of your ongoing daily experience. Again and again and again.

PRIMORDIAL LANGUAGE

So, what is to be done?
I'm suggesting a return to a primordial language.
One that exists as the deepest knowledge and expression that humanity knows.
It predates spoken language; it has its roots in the emergence of awe.
It is present in everyone, as an elemental music and reflection of molecular and stellar movement.
It is a genetic design built into leaf patterns and the bobbing of sea horses.
It is eminently present to children; we have educated it out of them.
But it is the story of our place in the universe and we must begin to tell that story again.
What we are losing is our ability to speak to the whole.
The songs of celebration, the poetry of praise.   - Anonymous

Our words are so powerful. The language we use can connect us deeply to ourselves and others. Words give us an opportunity to share what is inside. We praise, acknowledge, and honor through our words. Just as easily, our words and language can distance us from our truth and reality. We can use them to hide what is inside. Most of us speak without considering that our words reflect the beliefs we carry. So often, consciously or unconsciously, they disconnect us from ourselves and the world.

On our yoga mat we take ourselves to the place in the above poem. Without words, what is within transforms into art. Our truth shines, rises, and lives in the world. It is something we feel and experience – truly an emergence of awe. We leave feeling connected, whole. However, that feeling is often forgotten by the time we reach for our phone or engage in the next conversation. We lose our ability to speak to the wholeness we have experienced. In that space, we are often disconnected, ungrounded, and out of touch with our bodies. How many times have we spoken from that place – or continue to speak from that place – using words to fill space, to move away from fear, to hide what is inside, to not feel? Speaking from this place keeps things the same; it reinforces the same roles and behaviors, even when they cause harm.

I recently lost my ability to speak from my center, from my whole self. It gave me an opportunity to examine my motives around my speech. I found myself challenged to tell my truth, to share it in the world. I minced words, fluffed things up and beat around the bush. I habitually fall into these patterns with my words. Educated away from telling the truth, speaking my truth, I protect and guard with my words. It creates vagueness, a grey area where interpretation and assumptions become commonplace. I was conscious of the fear to write my truth, to stand in my truth. The words I wrote – my vagueness – created a deep disconnect.

My guarded and protected words seemed kinder on the surface, but they created no foundation of truth on which to stand or on which to build. They simply disconnected me from what was real; they were based on fears and emotional dependence. All of that was covered with too many words – surface words to fill the space of my discomfort, to keep my fear hidden, to keep me stuck. When it came right down to it, one simple sentence was all that was needed: no fillers, no protection, just simple truth.

I felt a relief well up and space open the minute that truth was out. The fear was still there, but moving forward through that fear opened me to an even deeper truth. Underneath the truth was an attachment – an attachment to the hope that the situation would be or was different. That was the truth I feared looking at. Held in the space of truth, the fear lessened.

As we ground and root and stay deep within ourselves, we begin to experience emotions and feelings, and with that, we begin to recognize truth. In this sometimes foreign place of our body, we can begin to trust and listen to the wisdom that is within. We will know when it is time to speak and when it is time to listen; we will know when it is time to say less. That truth, bubbling up from deep inside, creates a space of incredible freedom. It is our deepest knowledge and truest expression. When we find the courage to live in the space that is elemental and awe inspiring, we can trust that our words will come from a place of love. It will stem from knowing our place in the universe, it will naturally rise up and emerge through us, it will be the song of our life.

In seeking this expression of our truth, we can examine what we are communicating, how we are communicating, and what our motives are. In returning to our primordial language, we can ask: Are my words leading to wisdom and peace? Are the emanating the truth that I discovered within myself? Is it a simple, courageous expression of my truth?

Our words are so powerful. They are the way we express who we are in the world. Learning to speak with clarity, learning to share our wisest self, learning to be fluid in our communication is one of the most powerful, courageous things we can do. As we open to that space, truth spoken in a primordial language, the story of our place in the universe will rise up.

This continues to be my work in the world. At one time, I even affirmed out loud, 'I am a truth sayer'! With that comes enormous responsibility, much loneliness and a deep, powerful connection to me. This has become my daily commitment to myself, to the universe. And to tell this truth in the world, it must start with me. The river of denial must dry up! I know first-hand the power secrets have, how detrimental they are to our soul.

The body holds our truth, and when we deny the truth, it becomes confined, constricted, tension filled, anxiety ridden. The body seeks release. In our effort to protect and control, the dis-ease will find another way out. I like to say, 'It comes out side-ways'! Our body, spirit, whole being suffers. The truth truly does set us free! We free ourselves from the bondage of holding back, the body responds and lets us know where and how all the dishonesty, unshared feelings, and stifled words are held. We are then guided to release. It is a profound practice and one that is essential for us to rise to our most authentic self.

Contemplation to delve deeper in your process:

Consider a time you know you said too much, overshared, or spoke just to fill space. What was the discomfort? How did you feel, what beliefs arose, etc. How could the situation have been different with fewer words? What did you really want to say? What is your fear of sharing your truth in the world?

Breath practices to center, ground, align you in the moment:

Lions breath: Sit in a comfortable position, either kneeling or in a chair with your knees together. With your fingertips spread wide, place your palms on your knees or the floor. Inhale through your nose while keeping your mouth closed. Open your mouth wide, stick out your tongue, and exhale forcefully with a "ha" sound. Relax your face and take a few normal breaths. Repeat six times.

Actions to guide you to experience yourself as emPowered!

Tell someone what you love about them – be specific, yet succinct. Use three words.

Tell yourself how you feel. Make it a daily practice to name three things you feel.

Write out something you want to say to someone. Share it with a mentor or a friend.

Two prose specifically about receiving - an absolute challenge for me! Both opened powerful doors, ones that I continually want to close, to say 'That's enough!' Yet, I am committed to keeping these doors open. To knowing that my inability to receive cuts the fibers connecting me to you, me to everything that is. I remain humble, and hopefully gracious, as I keep the door of my heart open to receive.

IT TAKES A VILLAGE

I have always known this to be true. As a single mom, I needed and welcomed the village to help me raise my beautiful boy. My sisters were absolutely second moms to my son.

There are really no words to describe the help and support my parents gave me. Suffice it to say they were there every step of the way, from the really big things to the small everyday tasks of my dad picking Tony up from the bus stop and my mom making sure he had after-school snacks. Their home was where he felt safe and loved, supported and held, as if it was his own.

That is what a village does: it surrounds you where you are, creates a greater space of love and support to hold you, a space for you to grow. Today this proverb holds new meaning for me as it has expanded well beyond my immediate family.

* * *

I hurt my foot. I was sure that it was just a bad sprain. Broken? My mind said, 'No, not that!' The fear of my independence being challenged and even taken away felt excruciating. Thus, I protested, 'I think it is just a little hurt.' I now know that much of that denial arose from the thoughts *I have no one to help me . . ., how will I . . . .* - fill in those blanks with the many things I knew I would not be able to do.

I often speak about releasing our limiting beliefs. Those constricting beliefs are strong and resilient, very powerful. Mine so much that it took a break to release their grip, a break to create an outlet to discharge the pain they held. A short time before the break I became acutely aware of a limiting belief I was holding on to – my fiercely independent stance in the world. I began to observe how it was not serving me, how it created walls and defensiveness, an "I got this" attitude. I believe in the power of intention. As I became aware – willing to let go, ready to awaken – a space was created for the manifestation of that intention. With it came momentum, an impetus to begin the release. The energy flowed, walls broke open, the support poured in. My village arrived!

The village of my Wednesday night class surrounded me, supported me, and encouraged me to see a doctor about my foot. They held me in my fear. The collective concern and care for me helped me find the courage to engage with the truth. Yes, broken. No weight bearing. Seven weeks. I trusted. I softened.

You, my village, entered that space, surrounded me in ways I could not imagine, came in, and raised me! You watered my plants, drove me here and there, brought me veggies from your garden, and changed your plans to be of service. You brought me food, took me to the grocery store, took me out knowing I might be getting stir crazy. You called me, texted me, emailed me to see how I was. My fear dissolved in the arms of your attention, your thoughtfulness, your protection. Every single way you cared for me was precious, life changing. Waiting at the door of the studio to make sure I was taken care of, sweeping the floor, knowing what I needed and reaching out your hands and hearts to provide it. All the ways of attentiveness – amazing! You gave me a tangible experience of the power of the village.

This experience has expanded my vision of 'the village' immensely. It is newly spacious. I have been shown love in a new way. It is fresh and simple and dedicated and incredibly pure. Surrounded by that love, I stand a little firmer embracing my place in the world. Held in all directions, I have a new way of being fierce, an enlivened definition of independence, one that supports me more fully to be who I am.

I am forever grateful for this experience, for you, my village.

My wish is that your vision of 'it takes a village' expands. The invitation here is to join me in releasing old beliefs, deeply held patterns, so that in any and all moments of your life, you receive the blessing of your village. May you open to accept all that it will offer you.

My foot is healing, and I no longer need all the help I did. My heart is healing too. There I need you more than ever, as my village, to be by my side, to raise me and walk with me on this effervescent path illuminated before us!

This began an incredibly powerful journey of receiving. One which I am continually embracing. It gave me the experience of receiving from a place of vulnerability and openness. Prior to this experience, my old, very limiting way of receiving was to immediately start thinking of how I would repay you for what you were giving me. The realization that this was not receiving opened a door to my heart that had been closed, truly unavailable to me. The realization of the harm it caused my soul was quite profound. So much so, that my commitment is to stay in the vulnerable place, the often excruciatingly painful place, of letting myself receive. I feel so buoyed in this process, held as I recalibrate how to be in a world that offers me abundance and love and care and compassion and so much more!! I receive the gift receiving brings me!

Contemplation to delve deeper in your process:

What are the old beliefs you hold about receiving help? Who do you feel comfortable asking for help? Who will you accept support from? Who do you feel it is inappropriate to ask for help, to accept help from? When you do receive help, what are the emotions and feelings that arise? Who is your tribe?

Breath practices to center, ground, align you in the moment:

Acceptance breath. Find a comfortable seat. Begin to connect to your breath. At the top of your next inhale, sip in just a bit more. Breathe in the collective experience of love. Exhale, release separation. Continue this practice – breathe in, sip in more, experience love; breathe out, release - until you begin to feel your body soften, your breath deepen, yourself opening to the experience of receiving.

Actions to guide you to experience yourself as emPowered!

Make a list of all the things you wish you had help with. Pick three. Choose the top one. No matter how big or small, ask for help! Let the world in!

RECEIVING

Receiving – sounds like such an easy concept. Yet, this is where I struggle. I feel my strength is in giving. I receive greatly from giving, and have become quite comfortable in that space. I convinced myself that kind of 'receiving' was enough. That staunch stance was bound together with my many fears and beliefs about what it meant to receive. My unwavering position kept me from receiving the full goodness, the sweetness of my life.

Yoga teaches us to be in the grand flow of giving and receiving, teaches us to feel this through our breath, in our being, in connection to the world. I felt that the first time on my mat. Unbeknownst to me, my journey was opening me to connect to the art of receiving. Yet, often the messages of yoga are subtle, even elusive. This seed that was planted in my first practice lay dormant, sprouting only in the last few years. The sprouting of that seed has given me the opportunity to witness how frightening it is for me to receive, how I resist and side-step true exchange.

As I allowed the organic growth to open me, I watched myself planning how I would give back for what I was receiving. The discomfort of receiving was palpable, definitely observable. Rather than being in the grand flow, I would get stuck in the discomfort. Guilt would occupy my mind, along with thoughts that I needed to somehow repay the giver. I would experience the sense that I now owed this person, became indebted to them. This sense of indebtedness, this deep-seated belief, has been slow to dissolve. Its tendrils are widespread, twisting and coiling around my everyday experiences.

To become aware of our fears, our limiting beliefs, is a powerful force. Awareness becomes the ally of our healing, the ally of our highest self. This ally brings clarity in the moments of resistance. There, I witnessed myself and my inability to fully receive. With every bit of growth, as the old patterns of blocking would arise, I would try convincing myself that my lack of receiving was not harming anyone. Yet, blocking the natural flow of life harms all. It is a disruption of the most natural flow of our world. For me, it affects the way I hold myself in the world by sustaining the belief of undeserved-ness. It blocks me from feeling nourished, and it confines my soul, keeping me from being in the natural flow of my life.

As my awareness of this essential truth expands, a new foundation is created. The sprouted seed begins to flower! Wisdom arises - the natural current of life cannot be contained! The ebb and flow of all that is – love – is a stronger force than my refusing. With all my might, I simply cannot block the abundance, the love, the goodness of life. I can, though, create barriers so that rather than it being a swelling tide, it becomes a trickle. Release of those barriers gives rise for the slightly braver me to allow a greater receiving of the infinite flow, the conscious connection. Every day, as I become an invitation to open my heart and let the sprouting seed blossom, I witness the space of receiving widening from a trickle to a steady stream. Every time I receive, the powerful force of love moves through me. I see the possibility of easing into the stream of surrender, the possibility the magnificence of receiving offers.

My deepened practice with receiving has brought me very close to my own heart, as well as closer to Spirit. It has also led me to receive in new, abundant ways. I have experienced the potent force of love melt my judgments, the expansive truth of love hold my fears, the resilient supportive love dissolve my comparisons. This impressive force has not only brought comfort through both strength and fortitude but also in undemanding grace. It holds a willingness to meet me where I am, giving me in one moment the tangible offering of flowers and in the next the intangible mystery of the infinite. Sustained in my surrender, at ease with the natural flow, I have felt nourished in new ways.

The universe has so many gifts for each of us; so many possibilities await. We need only make ourselves ready and enter into the natural flow. I invite you to inquire as to how you may be refusing the gifts being poured into your heart, to consider how you are resisting receiving from this natural flow. I invite you to open your palms to the potent force of love flowing within and without all of us. I invite you to receive with me!

I continue to open to the blessing of receiving. I continue to learn how to receive. I remind myself again and again - I receive, I receive, I receive! As the many gifts -- in many forms, -- have been offered this last year, I have opened my heart to receive with a simple 'thank you'. What is essential is that this is followed with a letting go. It can be excruciating at times, while other times so fluid and joyful. I am learning. I am growing. I am in awe of this process!

Contemplation to delve deeper in your process:

What is your relationship with receiving? Recall a time you received something without attachment. How did it feel? Recall a time you received with constriction. How did it feel? What beliefs need to release for you to fully receive?

Breath practices to center, ground, align you in the moment:

Heart breathing - Sit so your spine is long and extended. Place your hands on your heart (sternum), one hand on top of the other. Close your eyes and focus on the space of your heart. On your inhale, stretch your arms out to the sides. Retain your breath. Imagine yourself receiving. Visualize a beautiful green spiral expanding from your heart, encompassing every part of you, and expanding in all directions from you. When ready, exhale through your nose, bend your elbows, and bring your hands back to your heart. Receive the moment fully. Repeat this practice six times.

Actions to guide you to experience yourself as emPowered!

Recall a time it was hard for you to receive – the gift, the compliment, the help. Pick one. Reconnect in writing or in person with the one from whom you received. Tell them thank you! Express that it was hard for you to fully receive from them in that moment. Now you have fully received – Thank you! I receive! Be in awe at the process!

IV

Change is the only constant in life, and the seasons have their own
unique way of remining us of that.
- unknown

Every season is one of becoming, but not always one of blooming. Be
gracious with your ever evolving self.
– Brittin Oakman

These next four prose give you a glimpse into my love of spring
and fall and all they offer. It still amazes me that I love them so,
despite their messiness, their unpredictability, and the way they
challenge me at every turn. I remain enamored and welcome the
encouragement for my growth. May it be for you too!

SPRING INTO SUMMER!

I planted a poppy. I have a vague recollection of putting it in the ground. As the spring sprouting began, I kept my eye on one area of the garden to watch its arrival.   As a poppy announced itself in another area, I hardly gave it notice, thinking it was one I already had seen, already knew.   One morning I walked about to greet my flowers and found that poppy had blossomed - a beautiful surprise, a most amazing opening, brilliance. Filled with delight, I giggled and exclaimed, "Wow!"

I have much to learn from this little flower! How often I live this way - looking in one area of my life - waiting, anticipating, expecting - where nothing is planted. Nothing is ripening, rooting nor growing. A simple turning is sometimes all I need to see the beauty in the moment.

I often anticipate and expect my process to look a certain way. Things are budding, opening, and expanding, yet I want to push them aside and disregard what they are bringing forth, thinking they are the same old thing, that which I already know. Sometimes, those same old things are still serving me, supporting me, and grounding me. Sometimes I am resisting my brilliance. Sometimes they just want me to let go. Sometimes there is a vague recollection of the seed within me, yet I forget what I planted and where I planted it. I forget my intention, my desire, my longing.

I invite you to reflect on this spring and last spring's offerings.   Ponder the ideas, inspirations, desires you were tending to, seeds you were planting. Look for expectations you have, ways you are looking in the same direction out of fear. Look for ways you have awakened, ways you have made shifts and expanded, ways you have opened. See that which remains and allow it to continue to serve you, to bring you joy. Reflect on your practice and how it has transformed, how it has delighted you. Rather than needing your spring offering to look a certain way, let it awaken within you, surprise you with its brilliance. See what new is blooming unexpectedly. You may giggle and say "Wow!"

And if not, look around. Sometimes the gift in blossoming lies in not seeing it in yourself, but watching as others see it in you and say "Wow" as they giggle with delight.

Spring! I love it so! Watching the world come to life. All the sprouting of what has been planted, all the new planting of what is desired to be created. Such a visceral experience, a tangible awakening. A place that fully supports our internal process of coming alive. From the fertile ground of winter, the possibility of seeds planted arrive. Meanwhile, the seeds of new dreams get planted, making room for what is yet to be dreamed. The sheer excitement often leaves us skipping a vital, essential step. Surrender! Surrender is the potent fertilizer for everything. Surrender creates within us the wonder, the awe, the 'Wow!' Yet, just like the poppy, our plans, designs, and expectations, our need for things to unfold a certain way, get in the way of the organic growth of our dreams. The time spent from the planting to the blossoming is ripe for our own growth. It's a season to learn to embrace surrender, to practice a daily reprieve from expectation and attachment. Full of moments to accept, to receive openly, and to release control. Moments to allow ourself to be surprised. Imagine growing your own wonder, your own awe, and your own joy! It is ready to spread through the garden of your heart, to intertwine with every dream, all your desires, all you have planted.

Contemplation to delve deeper in your process:

How are you resisting accepting life on life's terms? What are you attached to? What outcome are you longing for that is blocking your vision? What do you have expectations around?

Breath practices to center, ground, align you in the moment:

Three-Part Pranayama. Begin seated or lying down. Place your hands on your low belly. Breathe into the low belly, feeling it rise and fall. Repeat this three times. Place your hands on your mid-torso. Breathe into the ribs and the upper belly, feeling their expansion. Repeat this three times. Place your hands on your upper chest. Breathe into the heart center. Let the breath stream through this area. Repeat this three times.

For your next rounds of breath, combine all three: Inhale, breathe first into the low belly, and then pause. Expand the breath up into the mid-torso and pause. Inhale into chest, all the way to the collar bones or as high and full as is comfortable. Pause. Exhale, emptying from the collar bones down through the chest and into the belly, until you feel empty. Repeat three to six times.

Actions to guide you to experience yourself as emPowered!

Plant something. Tear up the papers from the contemplation prompt to use as fertilizer. Watch your seedling grow. Sprinkle it with JOY! As you water, it say 'I surrender to your growth, the way you are meant to be in the world.' Then, drink a glass of water and say that to yourself!

SPRING JOY!

Spring is unquestionably one of my favorite seasons. I am so enamored with the world coming back to life. I look with delight at everything rising – the budding of the trees, the sprouting of perennials, the tulips, the colors. The aliveness has me mesmerized.

This year as I watched with glee the early budding, spring surprised me in a new way. I found myself utterly delighted with the shifting spring weather . . . the rain, the sun, the wind, the snow, the warmth, the cold. I loved the way spring said, 'Wake up! Here is your surprise for the day.' It felt like an invitation to step into the unknown, to connect with the ebb and flow of life.

As spring was being itself, I was deep in my chakra workshops, opening new spaces and exploring fresh truths. I became very aware that my work was to find new ways to use my voice, accept my power, embrace new confidence, and surrender. What was yet to be revealed was how it would all come to be -- how spring, unexpectedly, would become my teacher.

Just like the changing spring weather, my work began to take on the same uncertainty. This was both on and off my mat. One day I was connected and moving with ease; the next day I was wobbly, winds taking me from my center. I thought I was going in one direction - sun, awareness. Yet, on the horizon, something new was forming – a bit of rain, dark and luminous clouds. Surprises appeared at each corner. Rather than being delighted, I began to find myself opposing the fluidity. The weather patterns of my life -- the unpredictability -- brought up fear. With the unknown so daunting, expectations arose about how I wanted to be surprised. By mid-spring, I was completely out of balance, fighting the internal weather patterns – resisting, avoiding, forcing, disengaged.

I had been dealing with mouth pain for many months. Despite numerous visits to the dentist, the pain and discomfort remained. I was angry and determined – I decided how it should be. I drew a line in the sand, unwilling to be surprised. Under the guise of finding my voice, owning my power, and being confident, I declared loudly that I would not be going to the dentist in April. No matter what! That posturing led to no delight, closed me off to any wonder before me. The declaration was made with rebelliousness. My eyes were closed to the fluidity. I pretended not to see what was right in front of me. I resisted, even dismissed, the season's offering.

Despite my defiance, spring persisted in her invitation into the unknown, continued to invite me to open to be surprised and delighted. Imagine my astonishment – me in the dentist chair in April! There, I called upon spring, sought the perseverance, the ability to be free and unattached. This led me to a miraculous place. My rebelliousness, my fear, began to soften, and a new unexpected weather pattern arose. I experienced

rain – tears flowing *and* a place to feel grounded;

clouds – ignorance, misperception *and* acceptance, the truth revealed;

winds – fears in many forms *and* a place of support to be with the moment as it was;

sun – clarity, awareness *and* my ability to embrace my power, my strength.

As the fluctuations moved around me, I was able to be present, able to make choices from a strong center. I felt empowered through surrender and open to the vulnerability that presence brings. My voice appeared in the most confident way.

As I embraced my power, my lack of faith diminished. I let go and surrendered into the unknown oscillations that I had been so desperately fearing, desperately fighting. As I surrendered, a profound, deep, and perfect peace arose within me. In that moment, the ground had me, and the ease held me. Suddenly, *I* was the beautiful spring rise and fall.

In wanting our practice, our life, and our work to be exactly as we have decided it should be, the surprise meant to awaken and delight us is lost. Happy and content only if things are exactly as we desire them to be, we miss the surprise. There is no place for revealing, no place to be delighted. Spring offers a place of balance, helps us embrace a beautiful middle where there is no *either/or* but rather a space of *and*.

When we embrace spring in this way, bring it to our everyday practice, the ground becomes steady yet malleable. In that place, we can be stable *and* comfortable in the moment, courageous *and* gentle, strong *and* open. We can welcome the rain *and* give room to slow, to cry, to draw inward. We can embrace the winds *and* allow the wobbliness to help us find our deepest center. We can stand powerfully *and* allow the experience to move through us rather than moving the experience. We can welcome the fluctuations, the uncertainty, *and* experience calm and ease. We can move beyond our controlling *and* allow an unfolding. We can remember who we are *and* stand courageous and vulnerable with life as it is. We can welcome the sun *and* let it show us our brightness. There we can be surprised and possibly even delighted by life. The hope of freedom and joy arises from our willingness to be fully engaged, alive in all the moments.

This became my practice – in the dentist chair and beyond. This potent place of *and* is spring's grand invitation. There all things can be. In the openness of the sky, the sun beaming, the clouds dancing on the horizon, I gather the flowers of the day in my hand. Smiling, I open my palms and breathe out.

The petals flow into the breeze. As the drops of rain begin to fall,
I hear spring's call to wake up . . . to be delighted and surprised.
To surrender to each moment as it is *and* just be!

Spring is truly a season to help us embrace our full human experience. It teaches us to be fearless in the face of whatever arises, recognizing all of it as a part of our process and experiencing the ebb and flow of our being in this human form. Spring reveals to us the reality of impermanence and helps us to more fully embrace the moment in front of us. I remain enamored!

Contemplation to delve deeper in your process:

What declaration have you made based on fear? Based on resisting the moment? How are you in denial of what the moment is asking of you? How do you want life to be different than it is?

Breath practices to center, ground, align you in the moment:

Expanded breath. Begin in a seated position. Find your breath. Notice the point of origination of your breath. Focus your breath on that place. Repeat three times. Begin expanding your breath from the point of origination. Inhale to the right and left, expanding your breath outward. Then, exhale and bring the breath back to the center. Repeat three times. Keep your breath expanding left and right. Now start inhaling to the front and back, moving your breath through the front body and through the back body. Exhale and bring the breath back to center. Repeat three times. Keep the breath expanding left and right, moving to the front and back, and begin inhaling above and below. Reach the breath below the pelvis and into the earth. Then, reach the breath beyond the crown and exhale back to center. Repeat this three times. Keep the breath extending in all directions – left and right, front and back, above and below. Return to your center each time. Repeat this last part six times.

Actions to guide you to experience yourself as emPowered!

Draw a picture of spring weather. Include rain, clouds, wind, and sun - describe through pictures or words what each means to you; describe what the weather patterns are bringing to you.

FALL CLEANUP

There is so much I love about fall – my birthday, the studio's anniversary, the colors, the sounds, the warm light of autumn. Yet, the moment the first leaf falls to the ground, the complaining begins. In spite of all I love, you will hear about all the leaves, the never-ending bags, the work. It is hard to hear the love behind all my petulant words.

So here I am again, in the midst of fall and hardly enjoying it as my focus is on my never-ending yard and leaf cleanup. More work to do. I wish, hope, for a windy day so that I can take the day off of raking. That hope becomes a begging. I ask random people, "Do you think it is too windy to rake leaves?" Seriously, this is all-consuming in my head.

One Monday, something shifted. It was windy, yes. Despite that, I thought, *I will go see what I can get done*. No complaining; no asking for a way out; no letting anyone know I was raking once again. No corroboration of my unwillingness.

The raking began as it has so many other days, yet something inside me had changed. Like the Fall hues, my color was new. In that moment, on that day, I began to feel the power of fall, all that it was offering me. As I was present for the many yard tasks, an amazing clarity arose. I realized the root of my irritability. Though I love fall, it is a challenging season for me. It asks me, calls to me daily, to let go. This offering to let go is right in front of me, cannot be hidden away, or even blown away. I want to hide, but fall calls me to awaken.

That day, that incredibly fulfilling fall day, I began to embrace its offering more wholly than I ever have. I had a face to face with my fears, got up close and personal with my resistance to letting go. The flowers that had bloomed in spring and summer brought me clarity. Letting go of them – and the joy they brought me – was a challenge. Most years, I do not cut them down all the way. It will be a long time before new growth returns. Selfishly, I need them to remain. I realized I was causing my beloved flowers to suffer by not giving them the rest they needed.   They were ready to grow inward, but holding their outward growth made the task more difficult. Yet, I hold on to those parts that are wilted, no longer growing. Something inside me feels it cannot endure the exposed, bare garden – the stripped ground reminds me of my own vulnerability, my nakedness that I try to cover.

The crispness of the day brought forth a freshness in my awareness. This resistance to fully letting go happens in all levels with my life – with people, events, and things. As I looked into the unprotected parts of me, I realized how very little I had really let go. I still hold and grip around the upward, outward growth – clinging to what has already faded, that which is complete, to remain. I let go a little, leaving something to hold on to. There are very few moments when I fully let go, cutting down to roots that which is ready to be released. I realized there, wisdom lives in the roots. The roots inform me of the lessons learned and teach me how to act more skillfully in the world, how to be more authentically me.

Every so often, on that profoundly amazing fall day, the wind blew new leaves on my just raked lawn, cleaned flower bed, and swept walk. I chuckled, recalling past frustrations. On that day, I realized that fall is just being fall. Doing what fall does best, it gently guides us to participate in the messiness of surrender – not neatly packaged, but unabashedly releasing.   What may seem like irreverence is, in truth, a humble offering, revealing the beauty and completeness of the moment. Leaves falling, one by one, only when the time is ripe.

Instead of my usual stance of head down, I gazed upward. I watched as the leaves delicately left the place they felt so secure, the place where their purpose was to bring shelter, shade, and cover. As they released from the tree, they danced gracefully in the wind. Falling to the ground with the utmost ease, they were ready to move on, to find their new purpose. Like the leaves, my release leads me toward my new purpose, into the new layers and textures of my life.

That day was so glorious; my heart could hardly be contained. A part of me wanted to hold on to it, this newfound peace, to figure out the exact circumstances so I could recreate it. I chuckled again. I looked around the yard, at the trees bare to the bone, at the surrendered leaves, at the cut down flowers and plants, and at the open blue sky. It was very clear I was the one out of place. All of nature, in that moment, called to me to unite with them. Another leaf let go into the wind. In that moment, on that most precious day, I felt a new beckoning from fall: 'Join us, release, give into the wind, to the moment. That is when the colors, the sky, the world are most brilliant. That is when you are most brilliant.' In that moment, on that fall day, just like the leaves, I let go and surrendered to the beautiful moment before me.

As I read this, I am filled with awe, with grace. This is the absolute process that yoga, living life on life's terms, brings us. I could not have known how this profound experience on that beautiful fall day was preparing me for a deeper letting go, a letting go of all I knew and loved. A surrender that seemed impossible, unfathomable to imagine. To close the studio, which I nurtured and sustained for twelve years, has been that for me. A cutting to the ground all that had previously lived – a release from the core of my being, leaving the roots remaining in the ground of my heart. I am trusting the process. I hear the call there as I let go.

Contemplation to delve deeper in your process:

What have you let go of (seemingly) that you still have ahold of?
What old beliefs are you still clinging to? What is your fear of
letting go?

Look around your life – at home, at work, in relationships. What
is asking to be released? How is that invitation being shown to
you? What needs to be cut down, stripped to bareness?

What does the thing mean to you? How does it feel to let it go?
What emotion arises?

Breath practices to center, ground, align you in the moment:

Viloma: Begin in seated position. Find your breath. Imagine a
ladder in your body, with the base at the pelvic floor and the top
at the throat. On your inhale, imagine you are moving up the
ladder (between 3-5 rungs). Keep inhaling till you reach the top
and the lungs are full. Pause. Slowly and smoothly exhale, until
the lungs feel empty.   Repeat this six times.

Actions to guide you to experience yourself as emPowered!

Write down what you can release. Go outside and open your
palms. Offer to the wind the thing you want to release.
Give something away – clothing, knick-knacks, memorabilia, all
that you no longer need.
Write a good-bye letter to someone or something.
Find a leaf to put on your altar as a reminder of how to let go.

LETTING GO

The world is transforming before our very eyes. Colors are appearing; leaves are falling. Numerous times, I have looked up at the mountains, looked around me, and stood in awe. In observing the leaves, the subtle hues and nuances of color, I am amazed at their process. Each leaf reveals its truth through letting go.

Fall beckons us to follow its lead to be revealed, to let our own colors be seen. Fall offers us the process of letting go, to let our truth be known. Certainly, I am fascinated by what I am witnessing, awestruck at the ease by which surrender is happening, and in the same moment, completely frightened and challenged by fall's invitation.

The leaves change, release, and fall with such elegance and compassion. Like the leaves, when I experience surrender, my body opens, my mind softens, and the feeling of freedom is tangible. Elegance, compassion, and more. In contrast, holding on to my fear of letting go, my body tightens, my words are controlled, my mind races. My whole being feels awkward, clumsy, and unnatural. My fear of letting go has me in its grip. My soul longs for the elegant, compassionate release of fall. The inspiration of the leaves urges me, calls to me.

The call from the leaves – fall's invitation – exposes the many hues, tints and shades, each layer waiting to be discovered and uncovered. As my colors emerge, my holding, my clinging, and my grasping is revealed. I see the red appearing as clinging to old relationships, past hurts. The orange reveals my hold around old beliefs and the hope that they can sustain me today. The yellow reveals my grip on the way things were, the way I hoped they would be, and the way I hope it will be. Seen through the lens of fall, these discoveries are opportunities for surrender. Seen through the lens of yoga, they are opportunities to witness ourselves. Seen through the lens of an open heart, they are opportunities for love to arise.

These opportunities bring us into a deep relationship with the season. We become held in the equanimity of fall and are revealed in the deeper, more subtle layers of our transformation. My layers reveal a very specific ask from fall: help me let go of the struggle, allow me to release my fear of being loved, and guide me in releasing my fantasy relationships. Allowing those nuances to be revealed feels both frightening and freeing.

Surrendering to my truth, becoming transparent and vulnerable, opens a space for love. In union, in full partnership, fall can then support me and bring me what I need to be in my process. As I accepted the invitation to release, new power arose with these words: "I create ease in my life," "I am safe to be loved," and "My life and relationships are rooted in authenticity." Fall brought forth support for me in the form of mantras! As I unite with the season fully, I realize the essentiality of my actions. I let go, I receive. I surrender, I am filled. I stand in awe, amazed at this process.

Fall's greatest invitation in letting go is to trust and to know and to love. To trust that knowing and allow love in! It asks us to be fully alive in the moments of life, just as the leaves are alive in their changing. As we practice surrender, we gain faith and trust in ourselves, in the world. Fall keeps looking for those soft openings, for those moments when we unite with the present, the moment that we become brave enough to let go. Love keeps waiting for us to release in the new color arising so it can pour through us and hold us so we can surrender again. In that space, surrender becomes receiving, and receiving becomes release. The elegant, compassionate, and continual breaking open so that the color of our truth can be exposed!

I invite you to stand with me and acknowledge the difficulty of letting go, and at the same time accept its necessity.

As fall holds us all in that space, may we realize under all the letting go, within all the receiving, there is love.

It seems I write about letting go a lot! Surrender and letting go are my constant companions on my journey. The most recent offerings have challenged me to my core. They have challenged every belief I have had about letting go, have challenged me to put into practice everything I have ever spoken or written about surrender. I have witnessed the color of fear arise in a plethora of ways, wanting to tell me to turn a different direction, to hold on tighter. Surrender softly whispers to me, urging me on, reminding me I am held and supported. In those moments, I allow it in, and the color of calm sweeps through me. It reminds me that resistance is futile. The process, the season of my soul, has a direction, the colors encourage me to flow. There every color comes alive, every color vibrantly guiding me, leading me, showing me. Grace.

Contemplation to delve deeper in your process:

What true color are you afraid to reveal? What keeps you from being authentic? What part of you do you hide from the world? How would it feel to show up just are you are? Who supports you fully in being you? What is your relationship with change?

Breath practices to center, ground, align you in the moment:

Extended exhale breath. Be present with your breath, noticing the inhale, the exhale. When feeling grounded, Inhale for a count of four (1,2,3,4), exhale for a count of four (1,2,3,4). Repeat twice. Inhale for a count of four (1,2,3,4), exhale for a count of five (1,2,3,4,5.) Repeat twice. Inhale for a count of four (1,2,3,4), exhale for a count of six (1,2,3,4,5,6). Repeat twice. Inhale for a count of four (1,2,3,4), exhale for a count of seven (1,2,3,4,5,6,7). Repeat twice. Inhale for a count of four (1,2,3,4), exhale for a count of eight (1,2,3,4,5,6,7,8). Repeat twice.
When complete, bring your breath back to a balanced count.

Actions to guide you to experience yourself as emPowered!

Create mantras from your contemplation. Take a daily savasana, and give yourself the gift of daily surrender. In that space of surrender (savasana), repeat your mantras. Watch the colors of you come alive!

These prose hold an essence of connection. One of remembering that we are interconnected, interrelated. One of living in an open-ended space. One of grieving in all the ways grief appears and allowing it to expand our love. Each holds a deeper possibility of living fully, of having that living arise from a foundation of vulnerability. The hope, the intention, that each brings us closer — to ourselves, to each other, to an understanding of our belonging, here and now.

MESSAGE OF PEACE

I thought it would be a Tuesday like many – taking care of business, running errands, doing a bit of self-care. It quickly turned from ordinary to extraordinary as I was invited to see the Dalai Lama! I immediately turned my car around, re-arranged a few things, and made my way to see this beacon of peace and love.

That love and peace was palpable even in such a huge arena. He was playful, honest, and beautiful. His message was simple, yet incredibly profound.

The Dalai Lama reminded us that we are all the same, all made of 'star stuff.' Everyone wants a happy life; everyone has a right to their desire of that happiness, for their desire of peace. Every being, every living thing. He spoke of the importance of knowing this and having an open mind – an open mind that allows in questions, questions that ignite effort to find an answer.

The questions themselves can be simple. Are we stepping away from humanity? Are we spinning stories in our mind that keep us in a place of self-importance? Are we in a space of old thinking, where division and differences prevail? How often do we live that way, in the space of that belief? It is so easy to pit you against me, to compare, to judge, to say that our differences are a relevant cause for separation.

These answers, profound in themselves, lead us to more questions. Are you courageous enough to be a new thinker where all thoughts lead to global unity and your sense of self is in union with all other beings? All those beings whose basic nature is compassion and joy? Can your sense of self be within a circle wide enough to include all?

In the space of love Dalai Lama offers, we see each other in our sameness, similar. There, our differences merely highlight our unique essence. The Dalai Lama has said again and again that we can pray for peace, but peace will only come through action. Actions that move us away from separation toward unity. Actions that will be known to us when we look inside ourselves.

Today, may we all open our minds, become new thinkers, and hear the message. May we be inspired and courageous enough to make it a daily practice to invite in the questions that will lead us to clarity and wisdom, to know the contribution we can make to bring peace, love, joy to our world. There, we become our own beacon of light and peace.

The levels of separation that have occurred since this writing are almost unimaginable. The divides are now chasms: the separation hardened through walls, the discord and disharmony claiming every space. Racism no longer covert, rights being denied and stripped away, divisive conversations — all of this keeps us moving further and further away from each other, away from peace. Yet, as I read this, my hope is rekindled. I know it has to start here, in my heart, in a place of courage and strength, as I ask myself the hard questions. In that space of truth, letting myself be guided back to remembering, we are all connected. Today I remember this: action is the key. My actions leading to peace are the key. I can start with forgiveness — or at the very least — begin to open my heart to the possibility. To find an action that says, 'I stand for peace' and in the same breath say, 'I stand for my rights as a woman, as an American, as a human being.' Maybe I first have to find union, unity between those two statements. To bridge the space in me that sees those as separate. Today, I vow again to create that bridge, to be a new thinker and a contributor to peace, and to magnify that day after day, breath by breath.

Contemplation to delve deeper in your process:

Ask yourself one of these questions daily:

Are you stepping away from humanity? Are you spinning stories in your mind that keep you in a place of self-importance? Are you in a space of old thinking, where division and differences prevail? How often do you live that way, in the space of that belief?

Are you courageous enough to be a new thinker where all thoughts lead to global unity and your sense of self is in union with all other beings, whose basic nature is compassion and joy? Can your sense of self be within a circle wide enough to include all?

Pause, get still, listen, and allow the answer to arise.

Breath practices to center, ground, align you in the moment:

Circular breath: Begin in a seated position. Find your breath. Inhale, visualizing pulling the breath from the lower belly through the base of the spine, up through the low back, through the spine to the back of your skull, and up over the top of your head to brow center. Exhale, visualizing the breath/energy moving from the forehead and down the front body to the low belly. Continue inhaling/exhaling, visualizing the circular pathway of your breath. Unending, continuous flow. Repeat six times.

Actions to guide you to experience yourself as emPowered!

Have the courage to take the action that was revealed to you in your contemplation. Make the call, begin the process of forgiveness, and create a bridge. You will know!

QUESTIONS

As humans, we love answers to our questions. From a very early age, we are trained to get a correct answer, find a finite solution, and work toward a goal. Our world encourages us to get it right. Yet, our lives do not always correlate with one right answer, one finite explanation. In fact, many times our lives are made immensely incomplete with one choice. We are infinite beings, and our lives are meant to be an immeasurable expression of our essence. Each time we try to force answers, or create a timeframe, we thwart our own unfolding. The confining and grasping are evident in our body, in our breath. We become held and restricted, disconnected from truth, living lifeless moments.

Recently, as I was teaching, these words arose from my heart: What if we lived our lives like an open-ended question? Imagine the limitless potential in the free flow of our body. When we are at one with our breath, possibilities arise openly!

This resonates even more deeply after spending a weekend in the presence of David Whyte. He encourages us to 'ask the beautiful questions,' such as

What brings you to life?
What are the horizons waiting for you?
What are the visions you have let go of?

These beautiful, open-ended questions arise from the part of you that already knows and has already felt the call. In this open-ended space, we are invited into a conversation with the deep soul questions that remain patiently awaiting our presence. We are summoned to move from the surface to the deep nakedness of our own being, to reveal our innermost desires, our authentic longings.

For the questions to remain beautiful and open ended, it is essential to stay in the process and allow answers to arise in the natural experience of the moments of our life. It is essential to create a space for flow — a space where each question, each inquiry, has room to breathe.

When opening to the fullness of your experience, fear may flow and sorrow may arise, but simultaneously you will feel wisdom, love, and peace. There will be room to shape a life that can distinguish the authentic you from the pattern of thoughts, beliefs, and old worn-out images; there will be room to move away from that which keeps you from living your most courageous life, from being boundless in your existence. These beautiful open-ended questions will create space for joy, grace, and the immeasurable. They will lead you to explore new frontiers toward profound revelations.

I invite you to take a deep breath, stand open-hearted, and allow the answers to arise open-ended. There, may you find fully lived moments guiding your sure path forward.

The great challenge of open-ended questions is vulnerability! Vulnerability is perhaps our greatest change agent. Often seen as something to resist at all costs, vulnerability requires of us our deepest strength, our bravest actions, and our hearts wide open in the world. This is the path to knowing who we are. By resisting our own vulnerability, we negate the very experiences that are here to bring us to life! To bring us to a state of whole-heartedness, awake, alive in this very moment.

Contemplation to delve deeper in your process:

What is your relationship with vulnerability? How do you resist being vulnerable? What action can you take to move toward your dreams?

Put each of the following questions at the top of a blank page. For a week, free write on each one:

What brings you alive?

What are the horizons waiting for you?

What are the visions you have let go of?

Breath practices to center, ground, align you in the moment:

Belly breathing: Begin lying down with your legs straight and slightly apart. Close your eyes and find your breath. Place both hands lightly on your belly. Inhale and allow the belly to fill up, hands rising gently. Exhale and release the breath, hands softening down. Continue this breath practice, belly rising on the inhale and belly softening on the exhale. Repeat this six times.

Actions to guide you to experience yourself as emPowered!

Affirm: I am powerful; I have the right to live the life I desire.

Take a step toward a dream, a new way of being. Make the call, apply for the job, register your business name, gather a group, post on social media. You can do it!!

DARING

My good friend said I should write about grief. I said, "Maybe next month." As the next month came and I began writing, I realized this would be an ongoing narrative. I share the beginning with you now ...

We, as humans, seem to make our natural processes feel unnatural. Many times, grief is something people do not want to hear about, talk about, or be in the experience of. Yet, grief is a genuine experience of our humanness, a natural process of our life. We all have an innate capacity to grieve. In my capacity to grieve, I am discovering much.

Grief is messy and challenges you to be with the most intimate, frightening, all-consuming parts of yourself. It dares you to be with yourself in your natural process. The rawness exposes your underbelly and feels as if you are wearing your skin inside out. All words, all actions come at you in an unprotected way. In that space of vulnerability, undefended, a new aliveness arises within every single experience. Feelings and sensations are heightened, and the intensity allows you to be with yourself, with life, in a richer and more intimate way. Perhaps everything is being stripped away so that a new skin — less protective and confining — can find a place around you, guiding you to a more wholehearted way of living.

Grief is frightening. It takes hold of you and seemingly will not let go. It takes you to places within your experience of life that most of us would not venture on our own, being beautiful, tumultuous, exhausting, and connecting at the same time. Though seemingly frightening and ambiguous, grief is safe as it is your own experience of the circle of life, of impermanence. If you let it, grief will hold you, caress you, enliven you, show you!

Grief is inclusive. It allows you to see the beauty in life, the pain of life, to know love and joy in a profound, encompassing way. In that space of love and loss, there is nothing anyone can say to make it better, nor should there be. We so often want to remove ourselves and others from the tangible experience life is giving us. Grief asks us to stay and be in life's fullness, to know both its grandeur and its depths. We humans possess this extraordinary potential, to stay and feel, to live and die. We hold within us the possibility to be fully within the circle of life, in the moment, with truth.

There are many opportunities in life to grieve - the loss of a loved one, a relationship, a job, a way of being. All life is shifting and changing and gives us occasion to be with this sacred, beautiful process. I invite you today to begin to open to your grief and all it offers. I invite you to step in to the fullness of your human expression. I invite you to dare.

Grief reveals the depth of your love! Truly. There have been many moments of grief since this writing – people, places, things. In whatever form, grief is a beautiful offering to us. To understand our profound capacity to heal, to feel, to be embraced, expanded, drowned in love. For any of this to happen, the anger must be experienced, accepted, acknowledged, and processed all the way through. We may know this, yet some part of us tries to resist, to dismiss this part of the journey. In writing this, I had a lifetime of anger to release. How grateful I am that my grief led me there. How grateful I am to trust the process and let myself be held there. One of my most powerful affirmations came alive there: I approve of me! It arose in my grief, through my anger, within my sadness, and in love. That affirmation continues to inform my process of healing today. It has guided me through moments of grief, of joy, of possibility. It has given me stronger roots and new affirmations, supporting me in my current grief of letting the studio go. The progression has been in one moment subtle and in the next transparent – I approve of me! I believe in me! I choose me! I know as I choose into my grief, more will be revealed. In the revealing, there is always more love.

Contemplation to delve deeper in your process:

What grief have you been afraid to feel all the way through? What are your beliefs about the grieving process? What could you do to more fully embrace your grief?

Breath practices to center, ground, align you in the moment:

Heart breathing: Begin lying down with your legs straight or knees bent. Close your eyes and find your breath. Place both hands lightly on your heart (upper chest). Inhale and allow the breath to rise into the upper chest, filling up completely. Pause. Exhale and slowly release the breath. Continue this breath practice, adding compassion on the inhale. On the exhale, release the heaviness in the heart. Repeat six times.

Actions to guide you to experience yourself as emPowered!

Draw a picture of your grief or write a letter to your grief.

Take an action to more fully embrace your grief (i.e., join a support group, talk to a therapist, find a somatic healer).

VI

Wild Geese

You do not have to be good.
You do not have to walk on your knees
for a hundred miles through the desert repenting.
You only have to let the soft animal of your body
love what it loves.
Tell me about despair, yours, and I will tell you mine.
Meanwhile the world goes on.
Meanwhile the sun and the clear pebbles of the rain
are moving across the landscapes,
over the prairies and the deep trees,
the mountains and the rivers.
Meanwhile the wild geese, high in the clean blue air,
are heading home again.
Whoever you are, no matter how lonely,
the world offers itself to your imagination,
calls to you like the wild geese, harsh and exciting -
over and over announcing your place
in the family of things.

– Mary Oliver

Inspired by this poem and my many years of holding it in my heart, this prose is a present-day musing. Truthfully, I am still the in process of all that occurred. How grateful I am that these words are etched in my heart — woven into my being — and have become a living experience for me. For me, in this moment, it stands alone.

THE WILD GEESE

I remember vividly the first time I heard Mary Oliver's words. I was on the ground, seated, sorting through papers. Had I not been seated, I am sure that I would have fallen to my knees. Her words cut through me like a knife. I was not alone in my listening, yet I could not make eye contact with the other person. Such was the shame that arose. I was stunned, felt exposed, and wanted to hide away.

At some point, I remember melting into the words of her poem, as well as David Whyte's soliloquy. As the shame assuaged, the embarrassment waned, I allowed myself to be held, in the sweet solace words can bring. I felt it in that moment.

As we grow up, we receive messages without knowing what they really mean: 'Be a good girl.' 'Be a good boy.' Unattended to, these messages become core wounds. They leave us feeling as if we must crawl on our knees through the desert for a hundred miles just to be seen as good—by the world, or perhaps just one person. When we hold the belief of not being enough, having to be good and feeling bad, we place unattainable expectations on ourself. This begins to guide how we live, how we inhabit the world. Defined by outside sources, this lack of self leads us to experience the world with a quiet ache, always left wanting. There is simply not enough; *we* are simply not enough.

The truth is the fight to be good in the world is one that many of us grapple with. It leaves us working hard, trying to will our way out of the prison of our limiting beliefs. The subtleties of our woundedness can throw us off balance in a matter of moments. We give away our power, lose our voice, hide our gifts, sabotage our success. No matter how much we achieve, we are continually falling short having to prove our place again and again. No matter how many people tell us they love us, we doubt that love. No matter how much we have, it is never enough to fill the emptiness inside. The manifestation of this wound is endless, its hold on us is ravenous. We succumb to the consistent patterns that pull at us. We forget our place in the family of things. That forgetting creates an unstable foundation. We try to hold steady, but the precarious ground gives way, like sand sifting beneath our feet. The insatiable desire creates a world that feels unsafe, a world that is threatening. The barrenness of the desert is felt heavy in our hearts.

No matter whose voice brought these messages into our world, they remain held in our cells. Hearing something new — words that rip apart the fallacies held as truth — can be completely liberating and can lead us to a path of healing. Words such as 'We are in this together' and 'Whoever you are, no matter how lonely, there is hope.' Words such as 'Your pain is my pain. I too have suffered, felt lost, judged myself, experienced a sense of lack of self.' Words such as 'I too yearn for love. I too desire connection.' Words that remind us, no matter how distant we are from Self, there is a path home, a joining back into the family of things, a remembrance of our own voice. That revelation becomes paramount for our healing. The message of hope, of connection, of being enough, melts the heaviness in our heart, solidifies the ground of our belonging.

The journey home begins there, with a consistent, diligent practice of remembering who we truly are. It requires patience to stay on the path of our healing, to remember we do not have to be good. As new messages arise, our mistakes become less defining, compassion for our wholeness grows, and our sense of self begins to come from within. Our woundedness slowly takes a new shape, a shape where we feel, know, and experience ourselves as enough.

We moved into our new yoga home in the spring. In the middle of the COVID lock down. Sixth months prior, as I planned our Spring opening, I had a fully different vision. A beautiful community gathering, all of us together in our new home. Yet, it was just me, the lockdown keeping everyone away.

Then one day, as I arrived alone at the studio door, a most amazing delight - wild geese waiting for me. Mom, dad, three babies – gathering, glancing, exploring around our new space, our new home! To get to watch them grow and observe their little family brought me much joy! The geese care for their young, keeping them safe, guiding them gently, and offering a daily reminder: you are enough. Reminding me daily, I am enough.

I heard this was an anomaly. That in all the years past, the geese had not had their babies here. I took it as a sign! A blessing beyond blessings, their beauty and power here to inspire us. I looked for them every day upon my arrival at the studio door. If they were not there, there were markings that they had been! I would arrive with my fears, my questioning sense of 'am I good enough,' my COVID despair. Their arrival, their sound, high in the clean blue air, would bring solace to my soul. Sensing their presence, I felt supported — ready to open the door with courage, not heaviness, and with wonder and awe toward all the possibilities before us, before me.

Though the geese have moved on, their essence remains. They leave us with a foundational reminder that we are not alone. To come as you are, let the soft animal of your body lead you home. To know that you do not have to be good; you already are enough. To take your place among the family of things, and again and again, to be JOY!

Many seasons have passed since this writing. The studio is now closed, the location no longer our home. That deep feeling of 'not enough' arrived in the transition. There were many days when all the voices of that wound would rise up and make themselves heard. Inevitably, on those days, I would hear the wild geese. Every time! Life happens. Things change. There are losses and grief, sadness and confusion. There is also much joy and peace! The wild geese remind us of that. The wild geese remind *me* of that. It is not about trying to be enough. It is about continually showing up to our life, remembering we are not alone. To be a as consistent to that as the wild geese are in the clear blue sky. There, all is enough. There, I am enough.

Contemplation to delve deeper in your process:

Where in your life does your 'not enoughness' appear? What do the voices of that wound say? What are your beliefs around deservedness?

Breath practices to center, ground, align you in the moment:

Box breathing. Find a comfortable seat. Begin to find your breath, breath in through the nose, out through the nose. Inhale for 4, hold the inhale for 4, exhale for 4, and hold breath out for 4. Repeat six times, working up to 1-3 minutes.

Actions to guide you to experience yourself as emPowered!

Affirm: I am enough – morning, noon and night!

Practice child's pose (balasana), seated forward fold (pashimottanasana), and supported bridge (setu bandha sarvāṅgāsana). Take each pose for 5-10 breaths, letting your body soften into the breath.

VII

Our deepest fear is not that we are inadequate. Our deepest fear is
that we are powerful beyond measure. It is our light, not our darkness
that most frightens us.
We ask ourselves, Who am I to be brilliant, gorgeous, talented,
fabulous?
Actually, who are you not to be?
You are a child of God. Your playing small does not serve the world.
There is nothing enlightened about shrinking so that other people
won't feel insecure around you. We are all meant to shine, as children
do. We were born to make manifest the glory of God that is within us.
It's not just in some of us; it's in everyone.
And as we let our own light shine, we unconsciously give other people
permission to do the same. As we are liberated from our own fear, our
presence automatically liberates others.
-      Marianne Williamson

Perhaps my most vulnerable writing, the following prose are
offered to you in hopes we all understand the sacredness of
being here. Being here, in this particular moment, in this
particular time, in this particular way. That you being in this
world is profound. That you are an integral part of the whole.
That you are needed! You are loved! You are!

SACRED JOURNEY

As I embarked on my yoga retreat in Colombia, there was much preparation, many conversations, and lots of deep pondering. I was asked multiple times if I would go again the following year. Not only were others curious, but I was as well; it was part of my own contemplation. My answer to myself — and anyone who inquired, for that matter — was that I was going to meditate on it while I was there.

My intention for the retreat was to hold space for open-ended questions, truths to be revealed, hearts to be opened. It made sense that I would bring that intention for me with this inquiry. I am not sure of the exact moment I received an answer — but somewhere, sometime along the drive, as we passed from town to town, gazing at the ocean and taking in the villages and cities with our eyes, I heard my heart sing out, 'Yes ,we will return.' I was a little taken back as we had not even arrived at our first destination; it had been a long day of travel with still much more to go. Yet, I knew, I felt, I sensed, and I did not argue.

Rather, I became more curious. What is it that draws me so deeply to this land? Why is it that I feel so completely connected in a country with a different language and customs than mine, to a land not of my heritage? Was it the ocean? Yes, she brings me much joy and peace - *we run toward each other in love.* Yet, I sensed it beyond my deep devotion to her. A follower of the sun since I can remember, I thought, *Maybe it is the tropical light, the brightness.* Yet, again I sensed it went beyond that. I left the inquiry open-ended in that moment.

Once again, I am not sure of the exact moment - possibly driving to the Medihauca pool or floating the Rio Don Diego River. Maybe when our guide, Juan spoke so passionately about the rivers and the mountains and how the very essence of them runs through us. In one of those many divine moments, my heart revealed the connection: Sacredness.

Everything, *everything* is sacred there - the land, the people, the cows, the butterflies, each tree, the ants, the water. Everything. In this land, no monuments need to be built; no special clothing needs to be worn. There's no need for fanciness. The roads to, the place arrived at, and everything in between is sacred. The everyday, the openness of the lives, the community — it is all sacred. Nothing is hidden or prettied up for our visit - the garbage, the poverty, the mangoes, the laughter — it is all here. Here for us to experience, to witness, to participate in. The sanctity is our direct experience of the moment - the imperfections, the flow, the tide moving in and out, the sun rising, the full moon illuminating. My soul knows this sacredness. When found, it immediately comes alive. It longs for this connection, longs to see and feel in this way, with divine eyes, in divine union.

In that moment, I realized that in my everyday life, I tend to hold back and tend to reign in that part of me. In Colombia, I could be more fully me. I could invite the sacred into every moment without need to justify or explain, convince, or even say a word. To be that unencumbered is in itself sacred!

In returning home, the gift I bring with me is the knowledge and wisdom of this sacredness. That you are sacred, I am sacred, and the moments we share are sacred. I return with a renewed commitment to answer the call of my soul and embrace the sacredness of each moment, to express it in my words, my actions, my beliefs. I return with a renewed commitment to let go of the reigns and let you know that on most days, I think of one or more of you. In those times, I open my heart and send out a quiet offering: *may love and joy fill your life*. I want you to know that I speak out loud to my flowers in my garden daily, and they hear me! I want you to know that I pray, I bless, I honor, I kneel, I chant, and I believe.

If you feel this longing, the place your soul is yearning for, I invite you to join me in allowing every day to be an experience of sacredness. I invite you to connect to the symbols, signs, and energy infused with meaning all around us, all the time. I invite you into the sacred quality of divine seeing, divine union.

I went back to Colombia four times. Each time, my heart deepened through the experience. Each time, I felt more aligned with the land, with the people, and with the customs. Truly, it was a home I longed to experience. On returning home from the last retreat, my heart said, "Let that be enough for now." I knew we would not be returning the next year. That was March of 2019. We would have planned to return March 2020. I now know that would have never been. The pure connection I received there guided me then and continues to guide me today. The experience, all of it, is etched so deeply in my heart. I remain grateful. Shall I return? Time will tell. The experience remains in my heart as I continue to trust the sacred process in all moments, in every day!

Contemplation to delve deeper in your process:

In what ways have you experienced your soul's longing for sacred connection? How have you tried to reign in that longing? What is the fear in letting yourself be free to experience the sacredness all around you? In making your life a sacred offering?

After your action of practicing at your altar, journal about your ritual practice.

Breath practices to center, ground, align you in the moment:

River flow breath. Begin either seated or lying down. Find your breath. Visualize a river and imagine you sitting on the banks, watching the water flow. Feel your breath like the river, a constant flow. Inhale, exhale. Allow the inhale to free the tension that is wedged inside of you. Allow the exhale to flow out, carrying with it the crumbling of tension, stress, and worry. Let the natural flow of your breath, in and out, dismantle any walls, any rigidity. As you watch the tension flow, let the tide of your breath bring in resilience, wisdom, and calmness. A continuous flow, in and out. Sacred breath. Sacred flow. Repeat for 1-5 minutes.

Actions to guide you to experience yourself as emPowered!

Create an altar. Find a sacred space in your home and place objects that are meaningful to you. This can be candles, pictures, crystals, flowers, leaves, etc. Create a morning ritual. Choose one practice to do at your altar and commit to it for one month. This can include breathing, meditating, journaling, saging, lighting candles, etc. Create space for a daily moment of silence and reflection.

OUR WORK

This last year has been a powerful journey for me. In the midst of all the changes, I found it hard to put words to paper. Where I usually find a flow, there was a stifling. I allowed a patient process and hoped I would one day write again. I am grateful to say, I awoke the other day, and these words poured out of me. I then found this quote, the perfect way to begin.

> *The work of a mature person is to carry grief in one hand, and gratitude in the other, and to be stretched by them. – Frances Weller*

Arms outstretched, expanded through the central channel of heart energy, I have opened to the fullness of my experience. The tension between the two spaces has created a beautiful place for healing, for transformation, for widening love. This is my journey.

Something happens when you suffer a loss. That which you love is ripped out from inside of you. What is left is a gaping hole. One with which you are asked to stand in the world. Vulnerable. Naked. Unclear of who you are now. You are asked to go on, to step into the space of the unknown without that which you have loved, without the comfort of that which has been an integral part of your life, part of your heart. The vastness before you, the emptiness within, leaves you feeling lost and alone, even desperate. Desperate to not believe this is true, to have it return, to know it again. Desperate to have the scattered pieces of you put back together.

And yet, there you are. A lonely state of standing in the new place, without what you once had, not knowing what is before you. You grasp, your fear takes ahold, you beg, you resist, you get angry. Deep sadness ensues, so you bargain, and do everything except the one thing you know you need to do: Be still. Be present. Be with the hollow abyss. Despite the insistence of the mind, it is safe for you to go there. Despite the fear that looms large, courage holds you there. Despite any lack of faith, love is there wanting to heal you, to guide you home.

Something happens there. You go on.

I have been living in that space for a while now. The whole process has asked for my patience, and my persistence has moved me over hills, through valleys, and across landscapes I have yet to know. The terrain has felt treacherous, daunting, and often I have wanted to turn around and run back. There, in love, I am gently reminded - that which I desperately long to run back to is no longer. In that moment, I am asked to trust.

Trust, such a powerful word, thrown around in the lightest of ways, truly without the gravity of its reality. Trust says that the need to know 'why' blocks your heart, that your desire for things to remain the same stifles your essence and your insistence that it be different holds you back from the miracles waiting. At this, feet are stomped, fists are raised, and a bubbling anger rises. Trust says, "Feel that, let it out, look at what is there, peek beneath the surface." To trust, you know the moment is enough, complete, whole. To trust, you know you will survive this. To trust, you truly know all will be well, all is well.

Something happens there. In trust, you surrender.

This moment — or really many individual moments of surrender — allows room for the cavernous hole to begin to be filled. At first you may try to fill it with the sameness of what has been lost. Yet, at some point, you realize that is unfulfilling. You are left feeling more alone. You realize this empty space will be filled through your healing. Surrender again. Trust. Let love fill you. All the natures, forms, and ways of love. It takes shape *in* you, and it takes shape *out* of you. It takes the form in your life that will help you grow through your grief. It leads you to the new ways to be you. The you that now lives on in the face of loss.

Something happens there. You become more fully you!

There are so many types of loss. Often, I have wanted to compare mine and say, in the face of everything, that this is nothing. And yet, it is mine. Comparing thieves the joy I am meant to experience by moving through it, by embracing my experience wholly. I still cry most days. I still need more rest than I can imagine! I still feel the pain of the loss. I still want to stay cuddled in a blanket for most of the day. I have somehow found the courage to remain in the process. In the midst of that, to show up to life, to open the door to what appears and who appears! To get out from under the blanket and be upright! To allow myself to live and be in this space.

Something is happening here. A clear vision of me is appearing.

So, I am keeping my arms outstretched, my palms in a tender hold, with grief in one hand and gratitude in the other. In that stretched place, I know I am transforming.

Something is happening now. I am sure to be blessed.

And blessed I am. In the most unbelievable ways. Ways that do not cover my experience, but rather expose it more fully. Ways that have revealed deep layers of courage and resiliency that I had yet to embrace. Ways that have yet to be known, fully realized! Deep, inspiring, life affirming ways!

Contemplation to delve deeper in your process:

Recall a time of loss. How have you been resisting diving into the loss? How are you being (have you been) transformed through your loss? Write about the experience, describe how proud you are of yourself, and remind yourself of your courage, making a commitment to your process.

Breath practices to center, ground, align you in the moment:

Bramari. Begin seated in a comfortable position. Gently close your eyes. Take a deep breath in. As you exhale, make a humming sound like a bee. Let the sound to be continuous, allowing a full, extended exhale. You can play with the pitch, moving the sound high and low, guiding it to different places in the body. Experience the vibration of your own sound! Repeat six times.

Actions to guide you to experience yourself as emPowered!

Stand, arms outstretched. Hold grief in one hand and gratitude in the other (use objects if you like). Listen. What action(s) does grief need of you? Take them! Make this a daily practice.

BELONGING

My spiritual connection is not something I care to hide from the world. I believe when people meet me, they sense it. It is the basis and foundation that informs all I do, all of who I am. Over the years, I have had many people ask me where it comes from, what I believe, how it is. It has been hard for me to fully describe, to put words to my experience.

Yet, I attempt here.

A disclaimer: I will be using the word God and the pronoun 'he' for no other reason than that is what feels right in this moment. I invite you to replace the words with any that work for you.

As I begin, know that there are many layers to my spiritual connection, more is continually revealed to me. This is the foundation on which it grows.

As a preface, I begin with the words of David Whyte! In "Self Portrait," he writes:

> It doesn't interest me if there is one God or many Gods.
> I want to know if you belong or feel abandoned.

Those words are the essence of my spiritual connection.

Knowing that, let's talk about God.

About all things grand and wonderful. About love and awe and the infinite possibilities of living fully. About presence and connection and being here.

Let's have this conversation that so many of us resist, the one that makes us brace, flinch, or flee the moment the subject is broached.

Let's take a moment to pause and breathe, and I will begin.

So often any talk of God is attached to religion, to dogma, or to a pre-formed set of beliefs you are made to adhere to. I have definitely been tied to the definition others gave me about God. Yet, there was something missing for me. The intellectualized version lacked anything I could ground into. I deeply longed for and desired the feeling of God. I realize now I was trying to connect with God through my finite mind. On my journey, I discovered God, and all that word entails, is fully realized only through the infinite space of my heart.

My journey to God — to opening my heart to deep, unbounded love — began with unpacking, redefining, and much releasing.

God is often referred to and taught as a determined entity. Fixed. Static. The God of my understanding is fluid, graceful, moveable, open, boundless. As I began to understand God in this way, I needed to look at the beliefs I held that defined God, that were holding me back from our relationship.

First belief to unpack - God does not have a list. He is not a wish giver or a determiner of who is good or bad. Holding that belief leads me to see the world through the eyes of judgment, see me as not being enough. My wish not granted, not getting what I want, tells me how I have not been good enough to receive. From there, I begin to compare, see what others receive, and tell myself I must have done something wrong. I say, 'This person's life is working out and look at how mine is not.' In the same vein, when things work out for me, I look out and see all that everyone else is doing wrong and even take a self-righteous, better-than stance in the world. This belief leads to separation.

Throughout my life, I experienced that separation, spent so much time feeling bad and trying to be good. I carried a heaviness of knowing that list existed and that I would be found out, would get the short end of the stick, and would come up lacking in the end. Though I knew of forgiveness — studied it, read about it, even sought it in confession, the block remained. A brick wall stood in front of my heart, refusing to let it in. Holding onto my unworthiness, my heart stayed shut. Certainly, I could not be deserving of God's love, of true forgiveness. Another belief to release. When I keep this old belief about God, I become so limited, and truly all the gifts coming for me were pushed away through my fear of receiving them.

To heal this old belief about God, about me, it took a huge shift in perspective. It took an opening of heart to receive such words as Mary Oliver's: "You do not have to be good, you do not have to walk on your knees for a hundred miles repenting, you only have to let the soft animal of your body love what it loves." Wow! That brought clarity. I needed my own body to heal, to experience the fullness of God's presence.

Yoga, coming to my mat, practice after practice, moving my body to the rhythm of my breath, little by slowly, those words began to permeate my well-preserved casing and began to seep into my heart and soul. As each old memory would arise, each old belief was recognized. Rather than fighting or pushing aside, I let them be, looked at them inquisitively, and offered the moment to show me. As I softened, sweet wisdom began to fill those spaces of discomfort. I felt something different — something that I had been taught about God but had yet to truly feel. Moments of peace, connection, love, and even a possibility of forgiveness. Not the kind of forgiveness that glosses over the pain and continues to hold onto it, but a heart awakening. A soulful rising of this possibility.

As I opened that space, something new happened as well: that deep longing, that empty hole felt full. The very thing I had been looking for my whole life. The very experience I had longed for as I was kneeling in the pew, my life falling apart, looking around and wondering why everyone else could feel it, just not me. A reprieve from the emptiness, the scars my trauma left. An ease in my being so different from the many bottoms I had experienced, so different from the dis-ease I carried with me every day. A place where the intellectualized God dissolved and the God that was me arose. Like sweet honey, a balm for my heartache, love poured through me.

I began to experience God in a new way. In relationship. As a BFF in the grandest way. I let God in, told him everything. Asked for guidance, listened. Began to develop deep trust and faith, not in an entity far away from me, but with that which was already within me.

There, clarity arose, God had not abandoned me, I had abandoned me. For so long, I used God as a pinch hitter, praying — well actually begging — for Him to get me out of this mess with the promise that I would never (fill in the blank)! Inevitably I would get out of the mess, keep my promise for a moment, and then go back to doing it my way. The cycle continued. To see God in this way, I could continually hold on to the belief that God was abandoning me, forgetting me. Only when I begged and pleaded, walked on my knees for a hundred miles, would He show up. As I began to redefine this belief, I began to see that it wasn't God picking on me, overlooking me, or forgetting about me — *I* was the one doing that. I was abandoning myself. And as I had been accustomed to doing, I looked outside of myself to blame anything and everything for the way I felt. That way, I could even blame God. I could claim my own unworthiness and prove that to God, to everyone.

Once I could see this pattern clearly, only then could I begin to shift. When I made a choice to act less than becoming, God would be there, I would be there, and every bit as importantly, you would be there. Rather than feeling ashamed in the moment or guilt-ridden over what I had done, little by slowly, I began to allow myself to simply be there — grounded in the moment with God, present in the world with you, and practicing forgiveness. Just as I am, just as it is. A powerful union, connection, sprouting of love. As that love grows, I have become less and less afraid of you, of what you think of me, of how you will perceive me, of whether or not you approve of me. Within that sprouting of God's love, I own my belonging.

This new relationship with God gives me the freedom to be a work in progress — ever learning, ever growing. It gives me room to be fully and wholly me! With each moment of exploration, my experience of God expands and grows. There, I get to make mistakes; there, love does not falter. I get to fall, and a hand is offered to help me up. If I act less than becoming, self-love and forgiveness meet me. God's love shape shifts with me, absorbed in all moments, in all ways.

When probed to describe God and this relationship, the only way I have been able to do so is to say it is 'Big LOVE'. By *big*, I mean expansive, all encompassing, wide, deep, infinite. By *love*, I mean a feeling of resounding connection, an indescribable peace — a knowing this moment. A pause. A sense of being seen, known, and wholly accepted. This relationship cannot be bought, sold, or coerced. It is the now. It cannot be clung to. It is found. It can be felt, experienced, and known through my heart. God is no longer a man in the sky or any entity at all. God is simply around me, in everything, everywhere, in every way. God simply is not separate from me. He is in my deepest place of belonging.

And just like any other relationship, it needs to be cared for, tended to daily. It takes a willingness to see God in all moments and all moments as God. It allows me to do the things I cannot do on my own, to forgive myself <u>and</u> to forgive you! Love me *and* you! Take leaps of faith.

There is no longer a score card. In fact, no longer a hope to be saved from my humanness. Rather a wish, an ask every day for God to take my hand, to walk with me, to show me the way to be the best version of me, the one God already sees. I receive that gift every single time I ask.

Now, let's take a moment, pause, breath, and you begin. I want to know about your belonging!

Truly, I want to know! In my journey to this connection, I heard something about spirituality: not only is it my direct experience with my Higher Power, but it is also my direct experience with *you*. Me – HP – Me – You. If I leave that piece of it out, so much is missing. I am here in this human form to experience my divine nature. Rather than transcend, to learn how to be in relationship to all that is. Yes, please! Tell me about you. I will tell you about me. Together we will create our world.

Contemplation to delve deeper in your process:

What does devotion mean to you? What are you in devotion to? How do you express that devotion? What does spirituality mean to you? What is your desire for your spiritual life? What conditions could you bring about to create devotion in your life? List three of your strengths. From there, create a vision of you. Include how you want to be in the present, what you want to create, and where you want to go. Write it down, draw it, paint it – let it take the form that is yours.

Breath practices to center, ground, align you in the moment:

Divine breath. Find a comfortable seat with your spine long. Find your breath. Begin drawing the breath in from the crown of your head, filling yourself with divine grace, love, compassion — whatever it is you need. As it enters, feel it as a sweet balm flowing through you, covering every part, igniting light within, and soothing all that longs for ease. Let it completely pour over you, through you. Receive it well. Let it saturate the whole of you, all the way to your roots! On the exhale, release anything — known or unknown — that blocks your ability to receive. Repeat six times.

Actions to guide you to experience yourself as emPowered!

Pick a trusting friend, a confidant. Share with them your spiritual connection, your doubts, the things you struggle with, and what you believe. Then, ask them to share with you!

The path itself is not a straight line; it's a spiral.
You continually come back to things you thought
you understood and see deeper truths.
- Barry H. Gillespie

The beautiful labyrinth of our experience, the depth and breadth of our journey, our path is unending, unlimited. It opens us to continually seek to know deeper truths, to know our true Self. Our path has led us here, ready to begin again.

My hope is you are continually inspired to open this book and let the page reveal your next step, your next beautifully profound awakening, to be inspired to remain on your path. My hope is that you do that again and again and again!

Actions

The actions are many and varied. Each an offering to give you an opportunity to ground more deeply in the practices. A few of the actions are yoga poses. Simple, uncomplicated postures to help you embody your experience. You need no previous experience with yoga, nor any desire to practice yoga. Complete in themselves, they will give you a taste of how to open, to experience strength, to feel sensation. To know your body as home.

Chakravakasana - Cat/Cow

Begin on your hands and knees in table pose. Find a neutral spine. Breathing in, tilt your pelvis upward, press your chest forward, melt your belly toward the earth. Heart leads here! Breathing out, round your spine, draw the tailbone down, chin toward chest. Back of heart opens! Continue to move breath by breath, undulating the spine.

These two poses have always been so powerful for me! I say 'if we all do five cat/cows a day our world will change.' Incredibly calming and at the same time invigorating, it is truly magical in the benefits it will bring to your life! To our world!

 Balasana – Child's pose

Kneel on your mat or blanket. Sit your hip back toward your heels. Knees either spread mat distance or closer together. Bring your head towards the floor. Stretch arms forward, out to the side, or behind you. Let your breath spread through the back body. Rest there for a minimum of six breaths up to several minutes. When complete, rise back to sitting with a straight spine.

I love to say that child's pose is a beautiful way to kneel and kiss the ground. A beautiful way to connect to the human and the divine, to rest, to ground and find comfort in the moment.

 Paschimottansasana – Seated Forward Bend

Sit with legs extended in front of you. Keep spine erect and toes slightly flexed toward you. Bend forward from the hip joints, keep your low back long and extended rather than curving. Place your hands wherever they land – on the side of legs, toward the front of legs. Focus on keeping spine long as you breath. Breathe a minimum of six breaths, allowing each breath to soften your whole being. When complete, use your arms to help you come back to a sitting position.

A beautiful posture of surrender, moving closer toward your center, to you, there is much to be opened as you allow the body to soften, first the hamstrings, calf muscles, then on to the more subtle layers surrender brings.

 Savasana- Corpse Pose

Lie down flat on your back. Stretch your arms and legs out and away from your body. Move around – fix your clothes, your hair, prop your knees, etc. – until you feel your body ready to relax into the moment. Gently close your eyes. Begin to notice your breath. Let it be natural, like a breeze moving through you. Your mind will begin to wander. See the thoughts like clouds in the sky, floating, you letting them be, returning to your breath, returning to you resting. Return to your breath every time the mind moves away. When complete, slowly roll to the side, pause there for a breath or two, returning to your seat, rested and ready.

This is the dessert of our practice. So profound, savasana has us lying still, released from our over-stimulated, hurried life. As easy as it seems, it challenges us to our core – we witness the nature of our mind, the pull of our thoughts, realize the challenge of rest, to let go, and in the same moment, how desperately our soul longs for this. I invite you to let it be your gift of awareness, coming home to yourself little by slowly.

 Setu Bandha Sarvangasana – Bridge Pose

Lying on your back, bend both knees and place the feet flat on the floor hip width apart. Slide the arms alongside the body with the palms facing down. Press feet into the floor, inhale and lift the hips up, rolling the spine off the floor. Press down into the arms and shoulders to lift the chest up. Breathe a minimum of six breaths, filling up front body on inhale, engaging back body on exhale. When complete, slowly roll the spine back to the floor, one vertebra at a time.

I love to say that in Bridge pose you are building a bridge to yourself.! A heart - open, wide spacious bridge, to come home to you!

Tadasana - Mountain Pose

Stand with feet hip distance apart, pushing them firmly into the ground. Spine long, arms by your side, crown of head lifting. Bring awareness from the ground upward, engaging muscles of the body as you move mindfully from feet to crown.   Stand strong, grounded, stable, capable, emPowered.   Breathe a minimum of six breaths, with each affirming what you need. When complete, begin to relax your body. Notice your new way of standing, being in the world.

A powerful pose any day, any time. Mountain pose brings you home! Brings you to the now. Leads you to remember your place here, remember your power, your resilience and how to hold softness around that strength.

Breath

Our natural breath is full, nourishing, liberating, uninhibited. Our natural breath is the way babies breathe, bellies expanding, relaxing as the breath leaves. We lose touch with this natural breathing through our life experiences, the stresses, overwhelm, disconnect. Patterns are created that leave our breath inhibited, shallow, shortened, tight. This type of breathing, distant from our natural breath, keeps us in a state of dis-ease, disharmony, disconnection. There, we are separated from our true nature. The breath is a mirror for what is happening in my life, illuminating when I am stressed, overwhelmed, distant from me. Connecting to my breath, learning how to breathe, listening to my breath, is the surest way I have experienced returning to myself.

The practices I have included here are simple ways to begin to deepen your breath. This life changing act is right at your fingertips! It can bring you to calm, connect you to your intuition, open your creative channel, and yes, bring you home to yourself.

Learning to breath, utilizing breathing practices one of the most challenging things we can do. It is in the same moment, the most profound catalyst for change. If you find the breath practices challenging, I encourage you to stay with them, find one that works for you and remain with it until you feel comfortable to move to the next. They will all be here for you when you are ready.

Contemplation

Journaling, reflecting, has been an essential practice on my journey. There is so much power in putting pen to paper (or pencil for me!!). The act of getting what is living in your head onto the page creates a softening, a release, unlike any other. My fears can dissolve, what feels overwhelming or insurmountable is now manageable. Day after day, word after word, wisdom arises naturally, solutions are uncovered, your highest self begins to be your guide. This takes time. Persistence. Diligence. Devotion.

The questions offered are here to be a starting point. You may answer them briefly at first, but find as you continue you have more and more to say. I invite you to allow your voice to be a constant inspiration for your journey! That is my hope for you.

Thank you for your profound words:

T.S. Eliot, four lines of "Little Gidding" from Four Quartets. Copyright © 1936 by Houghton Mifflin Harcourt Publishing Company, renewed 1964 by T.S. Eliot. Copyright © 1940, 1941, 1942 by T.S. Eliot, renewed 1968, 1969, 1970 by Esme Valerie Eliot. Used by permission of HarperCollins Publishers.

Barry Gillespie, permission granted to use quote from TRUTHFULNESS granted by Barry Gillespie.

Serge Kahill King, permission granted to use quote from the Serge Kahill King Foundation.

Brittin Oakman, permission grated to use quote from Brittin Oakman.

John O'Donohue, excerpt(s) from TO BLESS THE SPACE BETWEEN US: A BOOK OF BLESSINGS, copyright © 2008. Used by permission of Doubleday, an imprint of the Knopf Doubleday Publishing Group, a division of Penguin Random House LLC. All rights reserved.

Mary Oliver, "Wild Geese" from DREAM WORK: POEMS, copyright © 1986 by NW Orchard LLC. Used by permission of Penguin Books, an imprint of Penguin Publishing Group, a division of Penguin Random House LLC. All rights reserved.

Alexander McCall Smith, excerpt(s) from LOVE OVER SCOTLAND: A 44 SCOTLAND STREET NOVEL (3), Copyright © 2006 Alexander McCall Smith. Reprinted by permission of Vintage Canada, a division of Penguin Random House Canada Limited. All rights reserved.

Frances Weller, permission granted to use excerpt from the Frances Weller Foundation.

David Whyte, [*The Journey*], from [*Essentials*]. © [*2020*] David Whyte. Reprinted with permission from David Whyte and Many Rivers Company, LLC, Langley, WA www.davidwhyte.com.

David Whyte, [*Self Portrait*], from River Flows. © [2007] David Whyte. Reprinted with permission from David Whyte and Many Rivers Company, LLC, Langley, WA www.davidwhyte.com.

Marianne Williamson, permission granted to use excerpt from A Return To Love, 1996.

In appreciation to my students, past, present and future, for
showing up, rising to the moment, for bringing joy to all
moments of my teaching.